26 More OBJECT TALKS
for Children's Worship

by Virginia Ann Van Seters

illustrated by Jan Wimmer

STANDARD PUBLISHING
Cincinnati, Ohio   14-02864

**Dedicated to
Dr. and Mrs. John K. Durst, Sr.
for their faith in God—and me.**

Scriptures quoted from the *International Children's Bible,
New Century Version,* copyright © 1986 by Worthy Publishing,
Fort Worth, Texas 76137. Used by permission.

Contents

Page

Foreword and Introduction

  1 Why God Doesn't Want Us to Sin 5

  2 What God Looks Like 7

  3 The Most Important Word in the World 9

  4 Why We Have Sundays 11

  5 Why We Have Mothers and Fathers 13

  6 Hate and Volcanoes 14

  7 A Special Relationship 16

  8 What Belongs to God 18

  9 Why We Should Tell the Truth 20

10 Who God Wants You to Be 21

11 God's "Be Happys" 23

12 How Not to Be Sad 25

13 Why We Should Obey God 26

14 Why Jesus Was Always Good 27

15 Mercy 29

16 Pure in Heart 31

17 Peace 33

18 The Price Tag of Happiness 34

19 Blisters and Blessings 36

20 Cookie Jars and Life 37

21 God's to Do List 39

22 The Real Jesus 41

23 A Gift for Jesus 42

24 The Good Shepherd 44

25 Follow the Leader 46

26 The Most Important Verse in the Bible 47

Foreword

The author of this volume and previous volumes of object talks for children is offering assistance to ministers, church teachers, and leaders of small children. She is active in the teaching program of her own church. Her chief joy is telling others about Jesus and God's Word.

Her suggestions are practical. For instance, she even suggests in which hand to hold a prop to be used, and the exact words to say in emphasizing a specific point. Her skill and knowledge made this book one of her best.

It has been my privilege to work in the field of religious education for more than fifty years in local churches—as a seminary professor and in statewide church responsibilities. These years have afforded me the opportunity of working with curriculum materials as writer and teacher on all age levels.

I am indebted to Miss Van Seters for her sharing understandable spiritual truths with children in these ways.

It is rewarding to know the author and to see her or the minister in action with these materials.

Dr. John K. Durst

Introduction

These sermons presented here have complete instructions for delivery and any necessary recommendations for universal adaptation. They are written exactly as delivered, by a lay person, to show that, where more feasible, someone other than the minister **can** give them. All instructions are given in brackets.

1

Why God Doesn't Want Us to Sin

You must not have any other gods except me.—**Exodus 20:3**

Object Needed: A picture of a stop sign, preferably in color, cut from a magazine or drawn with felt-tip markers on an 8½" x 11" piece of white poster board.

(*Walk in carrying stop sign in your left hand, if you are right-handed, or in your right hand, if you are left-handed. Sit down and lay picture face down in your lap. Look at children and smile!*)

"Good morning!" (You.)

"Good morning!" (Their response.)

"I'm going to hold up something for you to see. (*Look around at all the children as you say this. That lets all of them know they are welcome and included. This is a very important concept to establish and maintain whenever you give one of these talks.*) If you know what it is, I want you to raise your hand."

(*Pick up stop sign and turn it for all the children to see. Several children will raise their hands. Call on the one who raised his or her hand first. This rewards good behavior and reminds the children you are in control. Ignore all attempts to answer without hand raising.*) "OK, (*Call child by name, if at all possible. If not, use some term of affection, such as son, dear, sweetheart—whatever you can*

5

honestly do.), what is this? Who can give me the answer?"

(*He or she will probably give correct answer. If he or she gives wrong answer, say, "Well, now, I can see why you would think that's what this is, but that's not exactly what I had in mind." Be gentle - always.*) "Does anyone else know?" (*When you get the right answer, proceed.*)

"That's right! (*Call child's name.*) This is a stop sign. (*Look at sign.*) We know that stop signs are put on roads to make people in cars and trucks stop - so they won't get hurt. Stop signs keep people from getting hurt."

(*Lay poster face up on floor beside you as you continue to talk.*) "Well you know something? (*You don't want a response, so keep talking.*) The Ten Commandments are God's stop signs. (*Emphasize your next sentence by pointing with the appropriate index finger.*) God gave us the Ten Commandments to keep us from getting hurt.

"The first stop sign says, 'You must not have any other gods except me.' This means that God should be the most important thing in your whole life, because whatever's most important to you is going to run your life.

"Now, suppose the most important thing to you in the whole world is money or pride or jealousy. None of these things can get us into Heaven. We can't take any of them with us when we die. And none of them even make us happy here on earth! But when we obey God's first stop sign, and make God the most important thing in our whole life, He makes us truly happy. The Bible says (*Emphasize point with appropriate index finger.*) it is God who will give us everything we'll ever need to make us happy.

"So the next time you (*Pick up "stop sign" again for all the children to see.*) see a stop sign, I want you to remember that the Ten Commandments are God's stop signs to keep us from being hurt." (*Lay poster back down in your lap.*)

Prayer
(*Ask the children to bow their heads and close their eyes.*)

"Dear Jesus, thank You for giving us the Ten Commandments. Please help us to remember that they are God's stop signs. In Jesus name we pray. Amen."

2
What God Looks Like

You must not make for yourselves any idols. Don't make something that looks like anything in the sky above or on the earth below or in the water below the land.—**Exodus 20:4**

Object Needed: A statue or figurine of someone or something the children will readily recognize.

(*Walk in carrying statue or figurine in a bag. Sit down and put the bag in your lap.*)

"Good morning!" (*You.*)

"Good morning!" (*Their response.*)

"I'm going to show you something, and, if you know what it is, I want you to raise your hand." (*Slip figure out of bag and hold it up for all the children to see.*)

"That's right! (*Call child's name.*) This is a statue of (*Mickey Mouse, a cat, a dog*). You can tell it's (*whatever*) because it looks like (*whatever*). Statues show us what someone or something looks like."

(*Put figure back in bag in your lap as you continue talking.*) "All of us have seen statues of many, many things. But nobody (*Emphasize by pointing index finger.*) has ever seen a statue of God. You know why? (*You don't want an answer, so keep talking!*)

Because there are no statues of God. There are no statues of God because the second of the Ten Commandments says, 'You must not make for yourselves any idols. Don't make something that looks like anything in the sky above or on the earth below or in the water below the land!

(*Put hands on your lap and lean forward with animated expression.*) "Wouldn't it be nice sometime when we worship to be able to look at God? (*Keep talking for you're on the brink of your main point.*) Well, we can look at God when we worship. In fact, (*Point index finger.*) we're supposed to look at God when we worship! But we are supposed to look at God with our (*Point to your head and then your heart.*) minds and our hearts. (*Repeat.*) We can see God with our minds by reading about Him in the Bible and thinking about what we read. (*Repeat.*) We can see God with our hearts by loving Him and letting Him love us. (*Repeat.*)

"You see, (*Point index finger.*) it's impossible for anybody to make a statue that would really look like God. God is bigger than anything we could ever make. He can be everywhere at one time, so how could we ever make anything that can be everywhere at one time? And God is (*Smile!*) more wonderful than anything we could ever imagine, so how (*Gesture with both hands.*) could anyone possibly make a statue as wonderful as God?"

(*Take statue or figurine out of bag again and hold it up for all the children to see.*)

"Remember when we said the Ten Commandments are God's stop signs to keep us from getting hurt? Well, that's why the second Commandment or stop sign says for us not to make any idols or any statues to worship. If we (*Point index finger.*) think of God as being smaller or less wonderful than He really is, we'll hurt ourselves by not asking Him to do really big things for us, won't we? We won't ask Him for what we need.

"So let's remember that the way to see God is with our minds (*Point to your head.*) and our hearts. (*Point to your heart.*)

Prayer

"Dear Jesus, thank You for being so big and so wonderful we can only see You with our minds and our hearts. Please help us to remember to think about You and to let You love us. In Jesus' name we pray. Amen."

3

The Most Important Word in the World

You must not use the name of the Lord your God thoughtlessly.
—**Exodus 20:7**

Object Needed: The word "GOD" written very neatly and clearly in large block letters with a crayon or felt-tip marker on an 8 1/2" x 11" piece of white poster board.

(*Walk in carrying the poster in your left hand, if you are right-handed, or in your right hand, if you are left-handed. Sit down and lay poster face down in your lap. Smile!*)

"Good morning!" (*You.*)

"Good morning!" (*Their response.*)

"This morning we're going to talk about a tiny little word that is really the *most important* word in the whole world. This word is (*Hold poster up for all the children to see.*) GOD." (*Steady the poster with your left hand and point with your right index finger, if you are right-handed, to each letter as you say it.*)

"It's just three little letters—G, O, D,—but (*Look at children.*) it's the most important word in the whole world. We've already learned that the very first of the Ten Commandments tells us that God should be the most important thing in your whole life because only God can make you truly happy. And (*Point with index finger for em-*

9

phasis.) last week (*Or, in our last children's sermon, or in our last object talk.*) we learned that God is (*Look around at all the children.*) much bigger and more powerful and much, much more wonderful than anything we could ever imagine."

(*Smile.*) "So that means that (*Point to word on poster.*) 'God' is the most special word in the whole world! And if it is the most special word in the whole world, than we should treat it nicer than any other word, shouldn't we? (*Nod head as you say next two words.*) Uh huh! (*Lay poster face down in lap as you continue to talk. It's important to keep talking at this point because you are about to make your main point.*) In fact, that's exactly what God's third Commandment tells us! It says, 'You must not use the name of the Lord your God thoughtlessly.' We should only say 'God' when we are talking to God, or when we are talking about God. (*Repeat last sentence.*) We should never say 'God' as an ugly word, or when we're mad about something." (*Repeat.*)

(*Smile! This is the best part.*) "Since the Ten Commandments are God's stop signs to keep us from getting hurt, this (*Hold up three fingers.*) third Commandment or stop sign says for us never to misuse God's name. If we use God's name to mean something bad, we will begin to think of God as being bad and that will hurt us. Because God is never bad, and God never does bad things. (*Repeat.*) We can totally trust God."

(*Hold up poster again for all the children to see as you talk.*) "Whenever we use the name (*Point to word.*) 'God,' let's remember God's stop sign that says we should only use God's name in ways that will remind us that we can totally trust God." (*Lay poster back in lap.*)

Prayer

"Dear God, thank you for being someone we can totally trust. Please help us to remember never to use Your name to mean bad things. In Jesus' name we pray. Amen."

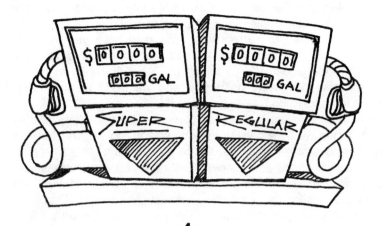

4

Why We Have Sundays

Remember to keep the Sabbath as a holy day. You may work and get everything done during six days each week. But the seventh day is a day of rest to honor the Lord your God. On that day no one may do any work.—**Exodus 20:8-10**

Object Needed: A picture of gas pumps. Be sure it's large enough and obvious enough for the children to recognize. Whenever you select props, always keep in mind where the children are coming from.

(*Walk in carrying the picture in a file folder or flat bag in your left hand, if you're right-handed. Sit down and lay the folder or bag on your lap.*)

"Good morning!" (*You.*)

"Good morning!" (*Their response.*)

"I'm going to show you something, and, if you know what it is, I want you to raise your hand. (*Slip photograph out of folder or bag and hold it up for all the children to see.*)

"That's right! (*Call child's name.*) These are gas pumps. Now, we learned in an earlier talk that for cars to run right they have to have gas, and, for people to run right, they have to have Jesus. (*The talk referred to here is 2 in 26 Object Talks for Children's Worship by*

Virginia Ann Van Seters, Standard Publishing, 1988. If you have not used this talk earlier, reword sentence above to read, "We know that for cars to run right, they have to have gas. And the Bible tells us that for people to run right, they have to have Jesus.") Since God made us to run on Jesus, if we try to run on anything else, we won't be happy, and we won't do the things we're supposed to do."

(Look at picture again briefly as you talk. Then look back at children.) "When we take cars to the gas station, do we only have to take them one time? *(Many of the children will probably say "No!" or shake their heads at this point. That's fine. Look at them, shake your head, and keep moving.)* Nooo, we have to keep taking them back on a regular basis *(Point quickly to photograph, then look back at children.)* to fill them up, don't we?" *(Nod head up and down. Then put photograph back in lap.)*

"Well, the same thing is true of people, too. We need to come to church on a regular basis and fill up our hearts *(Point to your heart.)* and minds *(Point to your head.)* with Jesus all *(Nod head up and down.)* over again! In fact, *(Emphasize next point with index finger.)* God who made us knew that we would need to come to church at least once every seven days. So, in His fourth Commandment, He tells us 'Remember to keep the Sabbath as a holy day. You may work and get everything done during six days each week. But the seventh day is a day of rest to honor the Lord your God. On that day no one may do any work.' This means that every Sunday God wants us to come to church to fill up on Jesus! Isn't that wonderful? You see, God thinks of everything, and He always wants what's best for us. So He made a special day for all of us to come to church so we can be truly happy."

(Hold up photograph again for all the children to see.) "The next time you see some gas pumps, remember *(Put picture back in your lap.)* God's fourth Commandment, or God's fourth stop sign to keep us from getting hurt, says we are to go to church every Sunday and fill up on Jesus!"

Prayer

"Dear God, thank You for giving us Sundays when we can stop working and come to church. Please help us to remember we can't do the things You put us here to do and be truly happy unless every week we fill upon Jesus. In Jesus' name we pray. Amen."

12

5

Why We Have Mothers and Fathers

Honor your father and your mother.—**Exodus 20:12**

Object Needed: A godly couple in your church who have at least one child. If you are married and have at least one child, use yourself and your spouse.

(*Walk in alone and sit down as usual. Smile!*)
"Good morning!" (*You.*)
"Good morning!" (*Their response.*)
"I have asked two friends (*Or my husband or my wife.*) to help me with my talk this morning."
(*Look at couple as you speak.*) "Mr. and Mrs. (*Call their name.*) will you come stand by me for a moment? (*Once they are beside you, facing the congregation, continue. Look at couple.*) Thank you! (*Now look at children and point to couple.*) I have asked Mr. and Mrs. Smith (*whomever*) to help me today because they are parents! Mrs. Smith (*whomever*) is a mother, and Mr. Smith is a father. They have a child named (*Give first name or whatever child is called. Or, say, "They have two children" or "three children" or whatever.*)
"Now, why do you suppose God made parents? Why do you suppose God gave children (*Point to respective parent as you say their position.*) a mother and a father?" (*You don't want a verbal response here, so keep talking. Also it's very important to say, "Gave children," not "God gave all children" or "God gave you a mother and a father." Not all children have both parents or either parent, and at no time should any of them ever feel they're different or left out.*)
"God gave us mothers and fathers to do two (*Hold up two fingers.*) things. (*Repeat. Then count off on fingers as you continue.*) First, God gave us mothers and fathers to take care of us. Mothers and fathers love us and give us a place to live. They feed us and give us clothes. They teach us things we need to know and always try very hard to do what's best for us. So mothers and fathers take care of us. Second, God gave us mothers and fathers to show us what God is like." (*Repeat from "God gave" on.*)
(*Emphasize by pointing index finger.*) "You see, it's really God

who lets our parents take care of us, isn't it? God loves us more than anybody in the whole world loves us. And God lets our parents love us. And God gives our parents homes for us to live in, and food for us to eat, and clothes for us to wear. And if we'll talk to God by praying to Him, He'll teach us the things we really need to know. And God always wants our parents to do what's best for us. (*Point to couple again.*) So, when we watch our parents, we see God's love for us, don't we? When we watch our parents, we remember that we have God, our heavenly Father, to take care of us.

"God's (*Hold up five fingers.*) fifth Commandment, or God's fifth stop sign to keep us from getting hurt, says, 'Honor your father and your mother.' (*Repeat from "honor" on.*) This means we are to listen to and learn from our mothers and fathers. You see, if we don't listen to our parents and learn from them, we won't remember to listen to God and learn from Him. And God knows everything!"

Prayer

"Dear God, thank You for giving us mothers and fathers to take care of us. Please help us to listen to and learn from our mothers and fathers, so we will remember to listen to and learn from You. In Jesus name we pray. Amen."

6

Hate and Volcanoes

You must not murder anyone.—**Exodus 20:13**

Object Needed: A picture in an encyclopedia, science book, or magazine of a volcano erupting in all its fury.

(*Walk in carrying the book or magazine in your left hand, if you are right-handed. Have a marker set at the appropriate page. Sit down and put the book or magazine face up in your lap.*)

"Good morning!" (*You.*)

"Good morning!" (*Their response.*)

(*See talk 1 for instructions on showing picture of volcano and eliciting responses.*)

"That's right! (*Call child's name.*) This is a volcano. (*Look at picture.*) Isn't it a furious looking thing! This old mountain has burned

and burned until it can't hold its fury inside any longer, and its really blown its top. And now (*Point to flowing lava.*) all that hot ugliness is going to destroy what's in its path."

(*Close book or magazine, with marker in place, and lay face up in your lap as you continue to talk.*) "We know that not all mountains are like that! (*Smile!*) Many mountains are cool and peaceful. They're the kind of mountains people like to have around because they're good for us."

(*Emphasize by pointing index finger.*) "Well, you know something? People are the same way. Some people are like that (*Frown.*) ugly old volcano. When they get mad with, or hurt by, somebody, they keep it (*Point to your heart.*) inside instead of talking to God about it. They get all hot inside, and they think about it. They get hotter inside, and they think about it some more—until finally they can't keep their fury inside any longer. Then they (*Spread hands to indicate an explosion.*) blow their tops and violently destroy whoever hurt them or made them mad. When this happens, it's called murder." (*Repeat.*)

"Now, obviously, murder is a very bad thing, isn't it? (*Nod your head and keep talking. You don't want to break their train of thought here.*) Yes. It's so bad, in fact, (*Point with index finger for emphasis.*) that God's sixth Commandment says, 'You must not murder anyone.' God doesn't want people to be like volcanoes. No. God wants people to be like cool, peaceful mountains. (*Smile and let it soak in for a very brief moment. Be sure to use the word "people" here instead of "us." You don't want to terrify the children*

15

into believing that when one of their friends get mad at them they're going to be murdered.) Whenever someone hurts us (*Now use "us" because here you are seeking to help the children find the proper way of handling their own hurt and anger.*) or makes us mad, God wants us to be cool and tell our feelings to Him so He can make us peaceful. (*Repeat from "God" on.*) Always pray to God about anything that bothers you. (*Repeat.*) Be cool and tell God your feelings so He can take care of your problem and make you peaceful."

(*Open book or magazine and hold up picture of volcano for all the children to see again as you continue talking.*) "So, the next time you see a picture of a hot old volcano busy being ugly, remember that God's sixth Commandment, or sixth stop sign to keep us from getting hurt, says, 'You must not murder anyone.'"

Prayer

"Dear God, thank You for letting us talk to You about anything that bothers us. Please help us to remember to be cool and to give our hurt and mad feelings to You so You can make us peaceful. In Jesus' name we pray. Amen."

7

A Special Relationship

You must not be guilty of adultery.—**Exodus 20:14**

Object Needed: Bride and groom off the top of a wedding cake. If you don't have one of your own or can't borrow one from a friend, use two dolls dressed as bride and groom, or a picture of a bride and groom. The most important thing is that the object(s) used be easily recognizable to children as a bride and a groom.

(*Walk in carrying bride and groom in a closed box - or photo in file folder or flat bag. Sit down and put box or bag in your lap.*)
"Good morning!" (*You.*)
"Good morning!" (*Their response.*)

16

"I'm going to show you something and, if you know what it is, I want you to raise your hand." (*Slip figure(s) or photo out of bag or file folder and hold up for all the children to see.*)

"That's right! (*Call child's name.*) This is (*Point to each.*) a bride and a groom. This is a man and a woman who have married each other. Because they have married each other, they have a very special relationship. (*Repeat.*) In fact, it is so special God wrote a whole Commandment to tell us about it. (*Emphasize by pointing index finger.*) God's seventh Commandment says, 'You must not be guilty of adultery.' This means that (*Point to respective figures.*) a woman and a man who are married are supposed to have a relationship with each other that is different from any other relationship in their lives. A man and a woman (*Put figure in lap, facing children, or stand photo in lap, facing children, as you continue talking.*) who are married are supposed to share (*Hold up two fingers.*) two things only with each other. (*Hold up one finger.*) The first thing they are to share only with each other is a very special love. We love our parents, (*Look around at all the children.*) and we love our friends, but when a man and a woman are married, they have a love for each other that is supposed to be different from any other kind of love in the whole world. (*Hold up two fingers.*) The second thing they are to share only with each other is a special kind of trust. When a man and a woman are married, they should be able to trust their hearts and their happiness to each other, all the time. (*Repeat.*)

"That's why God wrote a whole Commandment about marriage. This commandment is one of God's 'stop signs' to keep us from getting hurt. If we learn it as children, when we become teenagers

17

and begin to go on dates, we'll know what we're supposed to be looking for.

Prayer

"Dear God, thank You for making something as wonderful as marriage. Please help us to remember that a man and a woman who are married have a special love and a special trust they share only with each other. In Jesus' name we pray. Amen."

8

What Belongs to God

You must not steal.—**Exodus 20:15**

Object Needed: A picture from a magazine or book of someone who is very obviously a robber.

(*Walk in carrying prop in your left hand, if you are right-handed. If a book, see talk 6. If a photo cut from a magazine, see talk 4.*)

"Good morning!" (*You.*)

"Good morning!" (*Their response.*)

(*See talk 1 for instructions on showing a picture of robber and eliciting responses.*)

"That's right! (*Call child's name.*) This is a robber. Now, who can raise their hand and tell me what a robber does? (*Repeat above instructions.*) Thank you. (*Call child's name.*) A robber is someone who steals things or takes things that aren't his." (*Repeat.*)

(*Close book, or put picture back in folder or bag, and lay it face up in your lap as you continue talking.*) "God's eighth Commandment says. 'You must not steal.' (*Emphasize by pointing index finger.*) He knew that stealing hurts people in (*Hold up three fingers.*) three ways."

(*Count off on fingers.*) "First, we (*Point to yourself.*) get hurt if someone takes something away from us that belongs to us. Second, when we steal from someone, we hurt our own souls. (*Emphasize by pointing index finger.*) Stealing is wrong, and whenever we do something wrong, we hurt our souls. The only way we can stop our souls from hurting is to be sorry for what we've done and ask God to forgive us.

"But there's a third way stealing hurts us. What about if we steal from God? (*Put your hands on your hips and look amazed.*) 'Why' you say, 'how on earth can anybody possibly steal from God?' Well, it's God who gives us all our money and all our time and all our talents. And He asks that in return we (*Count off on fingers.*) give Him the first part of our money, spend time serving Him, and use our talents to honor Him. So, if we spend all our money and all our time on something other than God, and we don't use our talents to honor God, then we are taking from God something that is His. We are stealing from God.

"The next time you think about the eighth Commandment, or God's eighth stop sign, remember that when we take something that belongs to someone else or God, we hurt them, we hurt our own souls, and we hurt God."

Prayer

"Dear God, thank You for all the wonderful things You have given each of us. Please help us remember not to steal. In Jesus' name we pray. Amen."

9

Why We Should Tell the Truth

You must not tell lies about your neighbor in court.—**Exodus 20:16**

Object Needed: A picture from a magazine or book of a court-
house or a courtroom.

(*Walk in carrying prop in your left hand, if you're right-handed. If a book, see talk 6. If a photo cut from a magazine, see talk 4.*)
"Good morning!" (*You.*)
"Good morning!" (*Their response.*)
(*This is more of an adult prop than any of the others in this book. If you're working only with small children, you may not get a correct response. Be understanding; you're there to teach them not to test them.*)
"That's right! (*Call child's name.*) This is a courthouse/courtroom. (*If no one gets it right, say, "Now, that's a tough question, isn't it! Well, this is a courthouse/courtroom. You want to keep talking and not have the children dwell on the prop. It's your point you want them to remember.*) In court it is decided if someone has broken a law or not. (*Repeat. Look around at children.*) So you can see how important it is for people to tell the truth in court. (*Emphasize by pointing index finger.*) If you tell a lie in court, a good person might go to jail, and a bad person might not. If you lie in court, people will get hurt."

(Lay picture face up in your lap, as you continue talking.) "In fact, this is so important God wrote a whole Commandment about it. God's ninth Commandment says, 'You must not tell lies about your neighbor in court.' *(Repeat.)* We know that the Ten Commandments are God's stop signs to keep us from getting hurt, and God doesn't want us to hurt other people by telling lies about them."

(Put your hands on your hips and look amazed.) "Well, does this mean that court is the only place we have to tell the truth? *(You only want a mental response here, so keep talking. Shake your head as you say the next word.)* Nooooo. The Bible tells us God says, 'You must stop telling lies. Tell each other the truth'" (Ephesians 4:25).

(Close eyes and shake head as you say the next word.) "Whew! That sounds *(Look around at the children.)* really important! Well, it is. It's also *(Point index finger.)* very simple. Whenever you open your mouth, tell the truth. God does. He never tells a lie."

(Pick up picture again for all the children to see.) "The next time you want to tell a lie, remember how important it is to tell the truth."*(Put picture back in your lap.)*

Prayer
"Dear Jesus, thank You for not wanting us to get hurt. Please help us to remember, whenever we open our mouths, to tell the truth. In Jesus' name we pray. Amen."

10
Who God Wants You to Be

You must not want to take anything that belongs to your neighbor.
—**Exodus 20:17d**

Object Needed: Two pictures from a magazine: one of a woman with very curly and and one of a woman with very straight hair.

(Walk in carrying props in your left hand, if you're right-handed.)
"Good morning!" *(You.)*
"Good morning!" *(Their response.)*

"I have two pictures (*Look around at the children.*) to show you this morning. (*Pull out photo of woman with very curly hair. Hold it up for all the children to see.*) This is a picture of a lady with very curly hair. She had lots of curls. (*Put photo face down in your lap. Pull out second photo and hold it up for all the children to see.*) And this is a picture of a lady with very straight hair. Her hair doesn't have any curls at all." (*Put this picture face down in your lap, too, as you continue to talk.*)

"These pictures remind me (*Smile and look around at all the children. This is for all of them.*) of a story about two ladies who were friends: one had long, curly hair and the other had long, straight hair. Every night, the lady with curly hair put (*Close eyes and shake head back and forth one time as you talk.*) all kinds of stuff (*Point to your own hair.*) on her hair to make it straight. She wanted to have (*Make your eyes big and look serious.*) straight hair—like her friend!"

(*Resume normal expression.*) "And every night the lady (*Look around at children.*) with straight hair put curlers in her hair to make it curly. She wanted to have (*Make your eyes big and look serious.*) curly hair like her friend!"

(*Sit back a little and smile.*) "Well, finally, one night the two ladies looked at each other, and the one with the straight hair (*Smile!*) laughed and said, 'Aren't we silly! Every night we spend all kinds of time trying to be each other!' And the lady with curly hair said, 'You're right! If God had meant for us to be different than we are, He would have made us different than we are!' So the two ladies decided to spend their time doing good things for other people instead of trying to change themselves."

(*Emphasize with index finger again.*) "Anything we really need, God will give to us if we will spend our time being ourselves and doing what God wants us to do. (*Repeat*) God wrote a whole Commandment about this. God's tenth 'stop sign' says, 'You must not want to take anything that belongs to your neighbor.' (*Repeat.*) God always knows (*Smile.*) what's best for you!"

Prayer
"Dear God, thank You for making us just the way we are. Please help us to remember that You always know what's best for us! In Jesus' name we pray. Amen."

11
God's "Be Happys"

Those people who know they have great spiritual needs are happy. The kingdom of heaven belongs to them.—**Matthew 5:3**

Object Needed: A large smiley face drawn with a crayon or felt-tip marker on an 8½" x 11" piece of white poster board.

(*Walk in carrying the poster in your left hand, if you are right-handed. Sit down and lay poster face down in your lap. Smile! You're about to tell the children how to be happy!*)

"Good morning!" (*You.*)

"Good morning!" (*Their response.*)

"We've had a great time learning about God's 'stop signs,' haven't we? (*No, you don't want a verbal response so keep talking.*) And one of the nicest things we've learned is how much God loves us. (*Emphasize by pointing index finger.*) He loves us so much He gave us 'stop signs' or Commandments to keep us from getting hurt! We also learned God did that because He wants us to be (*Pick us poster and turn it for all the children to see.*) truly happy. God wants all of us to be truly happy."

(*Point to poster.*) "All of us would like to look like this all the time, wouldn't we? (*Again, keep talking, even if you hear a few "Yes"!*)

23

"Oh, boy"! or "Yeah"! responses.) Well, we can by obeying God's 'stop signs.'"

(*Wrinkle your brow and lay poster face down in your lap as you say the next sentence.*) "But what about when bad things happen to us? How can we be happy when bad things happen to us? Well, God knows everything, and God gives us everything we really need. (*Point with index finger.*) He gave us (*Hold up eight fingers.*) eight 'Be Happys' to show us how to be happy when bad things happen to us." (*Repeat from "God" on.*)

"These 'Be Happys' are found in the very first book of the New Testament, and they (*Look around at children.*) are what adults call 'The Beatitudes.' These 'Beatitudes' are God's 'Be Happys,' and the first one (*Hold up one finger.*) says, 'Those people who know they have great spiritual needs are happy.'" (*Repeat Beatitude.*)

(*Point with index finger.*) "You see, it's a sad thing when a person is so busy running his own life he doesn't know he needs God. And a lot of people do this. But when you realize you don't know enough, then you come to church and Sunday school, read your Bible at home, and you learn about God. And that makes you happy!

"So the next time you don't know something about God, or you don't know what to do about something, be happy—because that means you get to learn more about God! Remember: God's first 'stop sign' told us that it is God who will give us everything we'll ever need to make us happy. And God's 'Be Happys' tell us how to be (*Hold up poster for all the children to see.*) happy even when bad things happen to us!" (*Lay poster back down in your lap.*)

Prayer

"Dear Jesus, thank You for giving us God's 'Be Happys.' Please help us to remember that learning about You is what makes us really happy. In Jesus' name we pray. Amen."

12

How Not to Be Sad

Those who are sad now are happy. God will comfort them.
—Matthew 5:4

Object Needed: A fairly large color photograph of a woman comforting a child who is experiencing some kind of pain (physical or emotional).

(*Walk in carrying the photo in your left hand, if you are right-handed. Sit down and lay poster face down in your lap. Smile!*)
"Good morning!" (*You.*)
"Good morning!" (*Their response.*)
"This morning I've brought a pretty picture for you to see. (*Hold up photo for all the children to see.*) Isn't this nice? (*Keep talking.*) This is a picture of a mommy or an aunt (*Or, if hair is grey, a grandmother.*) comforting a little child who's sad. (*Point to picture.*)
(*Lay photo face down in your lap as you say the next sentence.*) "Remember last week (*or whenever*) when we said God gave us eight 'Be Happys' to show us how to be happy when bad things happen to us? (*Keep talking. A response at this point would break their concentration.*) Well, (*Hold up two fingers.*) God's second 'Be Happy' tells us how to be happy when we're sad! God's second 'Be Happy' says, 'Those who are sad now are happy. God will comfort them.' Isn't that (*Smile!*) wonderful? When we're sad, God himself will comfort us if we will ask Him!
"If we will tell God when we are sad and ask Him to comfort us, He will. He will make us feel very peaceful inside. He will remind us that He never makes a mistake, and that He cares each time we hurt. And when we read the Bible, God's words comfort us. So the next time you (*Wrinkle brow.*) feel sad, (*Hold up picture again.*) remember God's second 'Be Happy' and ask God to comfort you! Trust God." (*Lay poster back down in your lap.*)

Prayer
"Dear Jesus, thank You that we can trust You. Please help us to remember when we are sad, to talk to You and to read the Bible so You can comfort us. In Jesus' name we pray. Amen."

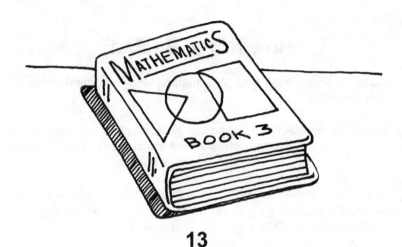

13

Why We Should Obey God

Those who are humble are happy. The earth will belong to them.
—**Matthew 5:5**

Object Needed: A school textbook for math that is very obviously a
textbook.

(*Walk in carrying the book in your left hand, if you're right-handed. Sit down and put the book face up in your lap.*)
"Good morning!" (*You.*)
"Good morning!" (*Their response.*)
"This morning I've brought something all of us see when we go to
school. (*Hold up book for all the children to see.*) This is a math
book. (*Stand book on your lap and hold with both hands.*) We study
math in school so we can learn how to count things, and how to do
business, and how to (*Tap the side of your head.*) think clearly."

(*Lay book down in your lap as you continue talking.*) "Now, imagine for a minute that (*Point to one of the children in the group and
call him or her by name.*) and I are in the same math class at
school. And imagine that (*Call child's name.*) likes school and really
wants to learn math. But let's pretend (*Frown.*) I think I'm so smart
that I (*Point to yourself.*) don't need to learn math. I don't' listen to
the teacher. When I grow up, I won't be able to get a good job or

take care of myself. That would be pretty dumb, wouldn't it?" (*No, you don't want a verbal response, so keep talking.*)

"Well, there's (*Point with index finger for emphasis.*) someone even more important than a math teacher we need to hear and obey. In fact, it's so important, God has written a whole Bible verse about it. Remember we've been (*Look around at all the children.*) talking about how God wrote (*Hold up eight fingers.*) eight 'Be Happys' to tell us how to be happy when we're sad. God's (*Hold up three fingers*) third 'Be Happy' tells us, 'Those who are humble are happy. (*Smile!*) The earth will belong to them.' Those who are humble are happy. That (*Make your eyes big.*) means those of us who obey God are happy!

"Some people think they're so smart they don't need God. (*Point to yourself.*) They want to be God! So they don't do the things God wants them to do. They don't obey God. They mess up their lives and can't take care of themselves. But God wants us to be happy. (*Smile.*) God wants to take care of us.

"The next time you (*Hold up math book again for all the children to see.*) think about going to school, remember, those of us who listen to and obey God will be happy. God will take care of us!"

Prayer

"Dear God, thank You for wanting us to be happy. Please help us to remember to let You take care of us. In Jesus' name we pray. Amen."

14

Why Jesus Was Always Good

Those who want to do right more than anything else are happy. God will fully satisfy them.—**Matthew 5:6**

Object Needed: None. The emotion in this sermon is better felt than seen.

"Good morning!" (*You.*)
"Good morning!" (*Their response.*)
"Some mornings when you wake up, do you decide, 'I want to be (*Smile.*) good today?' And other mornings do you decide, 'I want

(*Squint your eyes.*) to be bad today'? (*Keep talking!*) Or, are you good everyday? (*At this point you may get some verbal responses. That's OK. If someone says, "Oh, I'm good all the time!" say, "You're good all the time? That's wonderful!" and move on. If someone says, "I'm bad all the time!" or "I'm mostly bad," nod your head and say, "Well, you're going to like this talk!" and smile.*)

"All right, (*Hold up hands for silence if confessions are still pouring forth. Continue to smile as you move on because these outbursts show you've made them look inward and really see themselves.*) let's think about this (*Look around at children.*) a minute. Do you think Jesus was a good little boy? (*You will either get no response here, or you will get some 'Yes' answers.*) Yes! Jesus was always good."

(*Put your hands on your hips.*) "Why was Jesus always good?" (*Again, you may get some answers. Ignore the incorrect ones and respond to the correct ones. To "Because He was God" or "He was God's Son" say, "He was God" or "He was God's Son" and God is never bad.*)

"Jesus was always good because (*Pause very briefly here. You are about to make a major point.*) He wanted to be good. (*Repeat.*) Jesus wanted to be good for (*Hold up two fingers.*) two reasons. (*Hold up one finger.*) First, He loved God more than anyone or anything. And when you love someone, you want to make them happy. The Bible tells us that when we are good it makes God happy. So the (*Hold up one finger.*) first reason was because Jesus loved God."

(*Hold up two fingers.*) "The second reason Jesus wanted to always be good was (*Tap your head.*) Jesus was smart! Jesus knew that (*Speak deliberately here.*) God never makes a mistake, that God always has a reason for everything, and that God always wants what's best for us. He knew that if He always did what God wanted Him to do, if He was always good, He would be blessed. God's fourth 'Be Happy' tells us, 'Those who want to do right more than anything else are happy.' (*Repeat.*) So the (*Hold up two fingers.*) second reason was because Jesus was smart!"

Prayer

"Dear God, thank You for wanting what's best for us. Please help us to always want to be good. In Jesus' name we pray. Amen."

15
Mercy

Those who give mercy to others are happy. Mercy will be given to them.—**Matthew 5:7**

Object Needed: A large red heart you have made from construction paper, with a door cut in it. Have the word "Mercy" printed in capital letters so that it is visible only when the door is open. To make heart, cut out two large paper hearts. Cut door in one, then glue or tape "MERCY" on a piece of white paper behind door. Last, glue second heart on the back of the first so "MERCY" is indeed inside the heart. This works well when the door is cut with a razor blade. The thinner the cut, the better the door will stay shut. also, just cut the door in the heart. Do not open it until you actually come to that part of the talk.

(*Walk in carrying the heart in a large envelope or flat paper bag. Sit down and lay envelope or bag in your lap, unopened.*)

"Good morning!" (*You.*)

"Good morning!" (*Their response.*)

"This morning we are going to talk about God's fifth 'Be Happy.'

This 'Be Happy' says, 'Those who give mercy to others are happy. Mercy will be given to them.'" (*Look around at all the children as you repeat this deliberately.*)

(*Raise your eyebrows and put your hands on your hips.*) "'Mercy'? But what is 'mercy'? (*You don't want a verbal answer here, so keep talking.*) Well, there are (*Hold up two fingers.*) two kinds of mercy. There is your mercy for other people, and there is God's mercy for you.

"When (*Count off on finger.*) you give mercy to someone, it means you forgive them. (*Look around at children as you repeat this.*) When someone does something wrong to you, and they are sorry for what they've done, or they do something wrong to you because they don't know any better, the Bible says we are to give them mercy. We are to forgive them. We learned in an earlier talk that when you forgive someone (*Point to your heart.*) your heart forgets what they did wrong, and you give them another chance to be your friend. (*Repeat from "when." The sermon referred to here is 16 in 26 Object Talks for Children's Worship, Standard Publishing, 1988. If you have not used this sermon earlier, reword sentence above to read, "Now, the Bible tells us that when you forgive."*) And when you (*Carefully pull heart out of envelope or bag and hold up for all the children to see.*) open the door of your heart to let your mercy out, God will (*Put heart in your lap and open door, folding it back so it will stay open. Then hold it up for all the children to see.*) put His mercy in! (*Repeat sentence.*) When you are willing to forgive others, God will forgive you.

Prayer

"Dear God, thank You for wanting to give us your mercy. Please help us to open our hearts so You can come in. In Jesus' name we pray. Amen."

16
Pure in Heart

Those who are pure in their thinking are happy. They will be with God.—**Matthew 5:8**

Object Needed: A common, everyday product with the word "pure" on it—preferably one a child would use—but at least one he or she sees, such as soap or cooking oil.

(*Walk in carrying prop in a bag. Sit down and put bag in your lap.*)
"Good morning!" (*You.*)
"Good morning!" (*Their response.*)
"This morning I've brought a (*Lift prop out of bag and hold up for all the children to see. Name product: a bottle of cooking oil or a bar of soap.*) for you to see because it has (*Point to word pure on product.*) a very important word on it. That word is pure." (*Repeat.*)
"Pure means 'not mixed with any other thing.' (*Repeat.*) So if (*Point to product.*) this is pure, (*Name product.*) then there's nothing mixed in with it."
(*Put product on floor beside you.*) "You know something? (*Look around at the children.*) Pure is a very important word in your life, too. It's so important God wrote a whole Bible verse about it. God's sixth 'Be Happy' says, 'Those who are pure in their thinking are

happy. They will be with God.' (*Repeat both sentences.*) Now, we know that what we (*Point to your head.*) think about depends on what's in our (*Point to your heart.*) hearts. (*Repeat from "what" on.*) To be pure in our (*Point to your head.*) thinking, we have to have pure (*Point to your heart.*) hearts. And the only way we can have pure hearts is to let Jesus come live in our hearts! When Jesus comes to live (*Point to your heart.*) in our hearts—not just to visit from time to time—He (*Smile.*) fills our hearts! So if our hearts are filled with Jesus, there's nothing else in there, is there? No! When we have pure hearts, we are alone with God!

"The next time (*Hold up prop.*) you see a (*Name product.*), remember, when Jesus lives in your heart, you will have pure thoughts." (*Put prop down.*)

Prayer

"Dear Jesus, thank You for wanting us to think pure thoughts. Please help us to remember to let You live in our hearts. In Jesus' name we pray. Amen."

17
Peace

Those who work to bring peace are happy. God will call them his sons.—**Matthew 5:9**

Object Needed: A Christmas card with the words "Peace on Earth," or "Peace" on the front. If this is not possible, then one with angels on the front.

(*Walk in carrying card in an envelope. Sit down and hold envelope in your hand. Look around at the children.*)

"Good morning!" (*You.*)

"Good morning!" (*Their response.*)

"This morning we're going to talk about God's seventh (*Smile.*) 'Be Happy'! (*Repeat.*) This 'Be Happy' says, 'Those who work to bring peace are happy. God will call them his sons.'" (*Repeat.*)

(*Make your eyes big and look very happy.*) "Isn't that a wonderful thought? We can be called the children of God if we 'work to bring peace.' Now, why do you suppose our working to bring peace makes God call us His children? (*You don't want a verbal response here, so drop your eyes and look at what you're doing as you carefully remove your card from its envelope.*) Well, I've brought something this morning that will tell us why. (*Hold up card for all the children to see.*) It's a Christmas card that tells us what the angels said to the shepherds when Jesus was born. (*If no words are on front of card, reword last sentence to say, "It's a Christmas card that shows God's angels telling the shepherds about Jesus' being born."*) When Jesus was born, God's angels said, (*If words, point to them.*) 'Peace on Earth' or 'Peace.'" (*Repeat.*)

(*Lay card in your lap as you continue talking.*) "The angels said this because Jesus came to earth to bring peace—in people's hearts. When you let Jesus come live in (*Point to your heart.*) your heart, He puts peace in your heart. When you (*Point to the children.*) tell other people about Jesus, you help Jesus put peace in their hearts! (*Repeat from "when."*) And when you do this, you (*Smile.*) are acting like Jesus. Then God calls you His children, just like He calls Jesus His Son!"

(*Hold up card again for all the children to see.*) "Whenever you see a Christmas card, remember God's seventh 'Be Happy': 'Those who work to bring peace are happy. God will call them his sons.'" (*Put card down in your lap.*)

Prayer
"Dear God, thank You for wanting us to tell others about Jesus. Please help us to be children of God. In Jesus' name we pray. Amen."

18

The Price Tag of Happiness

Those who are treated badly for doing good are happy. The kingdom of heaven belongs to them.—**Matthew 5:10**

Objects Needed: (1) An object familiar to children, such as a pair of socks or a box of cereal, with a price tag on it; and (2) a large price tag, made from white paper and a piece of string. Have the words "ALL THE TIME" printed on it in large, block letters.

(*Walk in carrying props in a bag. Sit down and hold the bag on your lap.*)
"Good morning!" (*You.*)
"Good morning!" (*Their response.*)

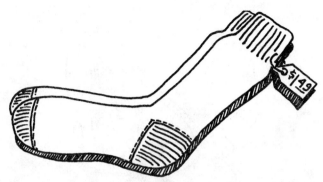

"This morning I've brought (*Lift first prop out of bag and hold up for all the children to see as you continue talking.*) a (*Name object.*) and on this (*Name object.*) is a (*Point out price tag.*) price tag. The price tag tells what something costs. (*Repeat.*) This price tag tells us this (*Name object.*) costs (*Name amount.*)."

(*Put prop on floor beside you - unless it is an object of clothing or something that should not be on a floor! In such a case, put object back in your bag.*)

"For the last seven (*Fourteen - however long it's been.*) weeks, we've been (*Look around at the children. You're coming to your key point so you don't want to lose their attention.*) talking about God's seven 'Be Happys.' We've talked about the seven things we must do to be happy. Well, (*Smile!*) today we are going to talk about the price tag on being happy! We're going to talk about (*Take large "price tag" out of bag and hold up for all the children to see.*) what it costs to be happy."

(*Turn tag, letter side up, toward you.*) "The price to being happy is (*Look at children.*) that you must be (*Speak very deliberately here.*) willing to do these seven things (*Read from tag.*) 'ALL THE TIME.' (*Turn letter side of tag toward children for all of them to see. Repeat your last sentence.*) You see, you can't be happy if you only live like Jesus some of the time. To be happy, you have to be willing to live like Jesus all the time." (*Repeat.*)

"So, the next time you see (*Point to "price tag."*) a price tag, I want you to remember that the price of being happy is to be willing to live like Jesus 'ALL THE TIME.' (*Put price tag in your lap.*)

Prayer

"Dear God, thank You for giving us Jesus. Please help us to be willing to live like Him 'ALL THE TIME.' In Jesus' name we pray. Amen."

19

Blisters and Blessings

Never shout angrily or say things to hurt others. Never do anything evil. Be kind and loving to each other.—**Ephesians 4:31b, 32a.**

Object Needed: A pretty shoe.

(*Walk in carrying the shoe in your left hand, if you're right-handed. Sit down and continue to hold shoe.*)

"Good morning!" (*You.*)

"Good morning!" (*Their response.*)

"This morning (*Hold shoe with both hands.*) I've brought something we all know about: a shoe. Shoes keep our feet safe and clean. But sometimes, when a shoe doesn't fit right, we get (*Wrinkle up face and close eyes very briefly.*) a blister! Or, (*Emphasize by pointing with index finger.*) sometimes, when we wear (*Look around at children.*) our shoes without putting on socks first, we get (*Wrinkle up face and close eyes very briefly.*) a blister!"

(*Put shoe on floor beside you. Then look at children.*) "None of us like to get blisters because all they do is be ugly and hurt."

(*Point with index finger.*) "But we all like blessings, don't we? (*Smile.*) We all like (*Look around at children.*) blessings because they're always nice things that make us happy! Blessings (*Point with index finger.*) are always nice things that make us happy!

"You know something else? If you took all the people in the world and got to know them you would find out that there are really only (*Hold up two fingers.*) two kinds of people in the world. They're either (*Count off on fingers.*) blisters or blessings. You're a (*Wrinkle up face and close eyes very briefly.*) blister if you go around being ugly and hurting people. But you're a (*Smile!*) blessing if you go around being nice to people and making them happy.

"Jesus was a blessing, wasn't He? The Bible tells us that Jesus 'went everywhere doing good' (Acts 10:38). But the devil is a (*Wrinkle nose and keep talking.*) blister because he's always being ugly and hurting people.

"So when you think about what kind of person (*Point with index finger.*) you want to be, don't be a (*Wrinkle up face and close eyes very briefly.*) blister. Be a (*Smile.*) blessing!

Prayer

"Dear Jesus, thank You for being such a blessing! Please help us to not be blisters. In Jesus' name we pray. Amen."

20
Cookie Jars and Life

But what a person says with his mouth comes from the way he thinks.—**Matthew 15:18**

Object Needed: An empty cookie jar or nothing at all. Cookie jars are usually made of some breakable material and can be heavy and awkward to handle.

(*Walk in carrying a cookie jar carefully in both hands, or cradled in your left arm if you're right-handed. Sit down and stand jar upright in your lap. Smile!*)

"Good morning!" (*You.*)

"Good morning!" (*Their response.*)

"This morning we are going to talk about (*Point to cookie jar.*) cookie jars!"

(*Look around briefly at children.*) "Mmmm! Do I see some smiles? Yes, I do! We like cookie jars! We like cookie jars because

(*Pantomime taking out a cookie.*) good things come out of them. And we know that good things come out of cookie jars because good things go into cookie jars."

(*Emphasize by pointing index finger. Look around at all the children as you continue speaking.*) "Suppose all of you were to come to my house one Saturday afternoon, and we were to make lots of cookies and put them in the cookie jar. Then when you put your hand (*Pantomime.*) into the cookie jar, good things (*Smile.*) would (*Pantomime.*) come out."

(*Again emphasize by pointing index finger.*) "But suppose (*Frown.*) you were to come to my house one Saturday afternoon, and we were to go through the house and gather up lots of trash and put it (*Pantomime.*) in the cookie jar. Then, when (*Pantomime.*) you put your hand in the jar, trash would come out!" (*Put cookie jar on floor beside you.*)

"Well, you know something? The same thing is true of our lives. When we come to church, (*Look around at all the children.*) our Sunday-school teachers and the preacher tell us we should say good things and do good things. (*Wrinkle up forehead.*) But how do we get things to come out of us? (*You don't want a verbal response, so keep talking!*) By (*Emphasize with index finger.*) putting good things in us!

"We can put good things inside our hearts and minds by, first of all, praying. We know that praying is talking to Jesus. We have already learned in another talk (*Talk 15 in 26 Object Talks for*

38

Children's Worship by Virginia Ann Van Seters, Standard Publishing, 1988. If you have not used this talk earlier, reword sentence to read, "We know.") that we can talk to Jesus about anything, because if it's important to us, it's important to Jesus! Just as we eat each day and sleep each day, we also need to pray each day."

(Hold up two fingers as you continue talking.) "A second way we can put good things inside our hearts and minds is by letting our parents, grandparents, or someone read the Bible to us every day, if we cannot read for ourselves. The words of God are the most important words we will ever hear, so we need to let someone read the Bible to us or read for ourselves every day."

(Hold up three fingers.) "And a third way we can put good things inside our hearts and minds is by doing what each of us *(Look around at them and smile.)* has done this morning. Come to church! When we come to church every week, we can hear the Bible preached and taught, we can sing songs about Jesus, and we can talk to other Christians. Coming to church every week is another way we can put good things inside of us!

"So, the next time you see a *(Pick up and point to cookie jar.)* cookie jar, remember: to have good things come out of your life, you have to put good things in!

Prayer

"Dear Jesus, thank You for making it possible for us to be good. Please help us to remember to pray, to read the Bible every day, and to go to church on Sundays so we can have good things come out of our lives. In Jesus' name we pray. Amen."

21
God's to Do List

If you love me, you will do the things I command.—**John 14:15**

Object Needed: (1) Very small pieces of paper with the words BE FAITHFUL printed on them. Have more pieces that you expect to have children. This is important. (2) A stack of 8-1/2" x 11" papers with your personal prayer requests written on them.

(Walk in carrying the stack of papers in your left hand, if you're

right-handed. Sit down and lay stack in your lap. Have small pieces of paper concealed in a pocket, or under your watch band, if you're wearing long sleeves.)

"Good morning!" (*You.*)

"Good morning!" (*Their response.*)

"Today we are going to talk about something grown people like to do. Grown people like to make 'to do lists.'" (*Sit back a little, make your eyes big, and look amazed.*) What are 'to do lists'? (*By now, if you've been going straight through this book, the children know to raise their hands if they want to answer something. If you see a raised hand, let that child answer.*)

"'To do lists' are lists of things people want done. (*Repeat. Then pick up stack of papers and hold in your hands as if you are going to read.*) I brought a 'to do list' with me. (*Look around at children.*) It's mine. It's my list of things I want done by God. (*Repeat. Then look down at stack and flip pages with one hand as you continue talking.*) It's pretty big, isn't it? (*You only want a mental response here, so keep talking. Look up.*) These are the things I've prayed about and asked God to do just recently. These are things I want Him to do for me, for my friends, for my enemies, and for people all over the world. I have things I want God to do each day!"

(*Put stack back in your lap. Look at children with a thoughtful expression and pose next questions in a quiet voice.*) "But what about God? Does He have a 'to do list'? (*Smile gently.*) Does God have a list of things He wants done by us? (*Don't wait for any kind of answer here. It will break the mood. Keep talking.*) Yes, He does."

(*Slip small pieces of paper out of their hiding place. Hold one up for all the children to see—with the words toward you. At this point you want to impress on them how small God's list is.*) "This is God's 'to do list.' (*Look at words printed on it.*) It only has one thing on it. (*Look at children.*) There's only one thing God asks us to do. (*Read paper.*) 'Be faithful.' (*Repeat.*) This means (*Look at all the children.*) that God wants us to obey Him all the time."

"And God has the same 'to do list' (*Give piece of paper to each child present.*) for everybody. 'Be faithful.'" (*Since each child has a list in his or her hand, and you still have some in your hand, this illustrates that there is indeed the same list for each of us!*)

Prayer

"Dear God, thank You for listening to our 'to do lists.' Please help us to obey You all the time. In Jesus' name we pray. Amen."

22

The Real Jesus

This is my Son and I love him. I am very well pleased with him.
—**Matthew 3:17b**

Object Needed: A copy of the Bible. Be sure it is bound in such a way as to be instantly recognizable as being a Bible.

(*Walk in carrying Bible in your left hand, if you're right-handed. Sit down and lay Bible face up in your lap. Look at children.*)
"Good morning!" (*You.*)
"Good morning!" (*Their response.*)
"This morning I want you to help me by pretending something. I want you to pretend you're new here at this church. You've heard about a person named (*Call the first and last names of one of the children most of the other children will recognize. Be sure it is a child whose father is still living.*), but you don't know him."
(*Again, emphasize by pointing index finger.*) "If you wanted to know who (*Name.*) was, you would ask his father. His father lives with him, spends time with him, and does things with him. So his father knows him.
"Then, if you decided you wanted to really get to know (*Name.*), you would go and talk to (*Name.*) himself. You would do things with

41

him and spend time with him. Then you would know him."

(*Look around at the children as you say next two sentences.*) "Well, you know something? The same thing is true about Jesus. If you want to know who Jesus is, you don't ask someone who doesn't know Him. Some people think you can read any book or see any movie if you want to know about Jesus. But you can't! Someone who doesn't know Jesus can only tell you lies or nothing at all.

"If you want to know who Jesus really is, ask His Father. God is Jesus' Father, and He has written a whole book about Him. (*Pick up Bible and hold it for all the children to see as you say next sentence.*) That book is called the Bible. Find out what the Bible says about Jesus. (*Lay Bible reverently back in your lap as you continue talking.*) Then go and talk to Jesus in prayer. And do the kinds of things Jesus would do. Spend time with Jesus—and then you'll know who He really is!

Prayer

"Dear God, thank You for telling us the truth about Jesus. Please help us to read your Bible and talk to Jesus and spend time with Him. In Jesus' name we pray. Amen."

23

A Gift for Jesus

Give to Caesar the things that are Caesar's. And give to God the things that are God's.—**Matthew 22:21b**

Note: This sermon may be used at Christmas.

Object Needed: The words I LOVE JESUS written very neatly and clearly with a felt-tip pen or a crayon, in large block letters on a large red heart you have bought or made from cardboard or construction paper. If used at Christmas, put heart in a gift box that can be easily unwrapped. Have a tag on the outside that says, "To Jesus."

(*Walk in carrying the heart in a file folder, flat bag, or gift box in your left hand, if you're right-handed. Sit down and put folder, bag, or box on your lap.*)

"Good morning!" (*You.*)

"Good morning!" (*Their response.*)

"This morning we're going to answer (*Look around at the children.*) a very important question. (*Pause very briefly to let your words sink in.*) This morning we're going to find out how good we are (*Look around at children.*) at being (*Speak very deliberately here.*) friends to Jesus. We learned in another talk that Jesus is our very (*Speak deliberately here.*) best friend. (*Talk 8 in 22 Object Talks for Children's Worship, Standard Publishing, 1986. If you have not used this sermon earlier, reword sentence above to read, "The Bible tells us that Jesus is."*) Jesus is our very best friend (*Count off on fingers.*) because He always makes us feel better when we (*Look around at children.*) talk to Him in prayer, because He lets us talk to Him about anything at all, and because He lets us share our bad times and our good times with Him!"

(*Hold up gift box, if using this at Christmas. If not, just keep talking.*) "At Christmas, and on birthdays, we think about our friends, and we want to give them presents. (*Put gift box back on lap.*) We want to give them something to make them happy.

"Well, there's something each of us can give our best friend Jesus. It's the (*Hold up one finger.*) most important thing we can give Him! (*Open gift box or folder or bag and gently take out heart.*

43

Hold it up carefully for all the children to see.) Each of us can give Jesus our heart! (*Smile.*) Isn't that wonderful? Jesus loves us so much He just wants us to love Him!

"Does Jesus deserve our love? (*Some of the children will proba- bly say "Yes!" And one or two little boys may say "No" just to see if they can rattle you. If there are only "No's" or nothing at all, ignore the "No's" and nod your head.*) "Yes, Jesus deserves our love! Jesus left Heaven and came to earth to show us how to live. He died on a cross (*Look around at children.*) so we could go to Heaven when we die. And He looks after us now and loves us more than we can even understand. (*Nod your head.*) Jesus deserves our love."

(*Pick up heart again and hold with both hands as though it's very precious.*) "So the next time you think about Jesus and how much He loves you, think about giving Jesus your heart!"

Prayer

"Dear Jesus, thank You for loving us enough to want us to go to Heaven. Please help us to love you enough to give You our hearts. In Jesus' name we pray. Amen."

24
The Good Shepherd

I am the good shepherd.—**John 10:11**

Object Needed: A picture from a child's Bible storybook, Sunday-school paper, or Christmas card of a shepherd or shepherds tending their sheep.

(*Walk in carrying book with page marked, or card or picture in an envelope. Sit down and put book or envelope in your lap. Look around at the children.*)

"Good morning!" (*You.*)

"Good morning!" (*Their response.*)

"This morning I've brought a very nice picture for you to see! (*Take card or picture out of envelope or open book and hold up for all the children to see.*) This is a picture we see a lot in church, es- pecially at Christmas time. It's a picture of a shepherd (*shepherds*) taking care of his (*their*) sheep. This is such a nice picture because

44

it reminds us (*Smile.*) of Jesus. In the Bible, in John 10:11, Jesus calls himself 'The Good Shepherd.' And in other verses in the Bible, (*Look around at the children.*) Jesus talks about (*Indicate everyone with a circular motion using your free hand.*) all of us being sheep and His being (*Point to one of the shepherds in your picture.*) our Shepherd."

(*Lay picture face up in your lap.*) "Jesus had a good reason (*Look around at children.*) for calling us 'sheep' and himself our 'shepherd.' You see, sheep are totally lost by themselves. The shepherd has to take care of them. The shepherd feeds his sheep, protects them, and makes them feel better when they are scared. And that's (*Emphasize by pointing index finger.*) exactly the way we are! People are totally lost without Jesus. (*Repeat.*) No one can go to Heaven without Jesus. And Jesus takes care of us. He feeds our bodies and our (*Point to your head.*) minds. When we trust Him, the way a sheep trusts his shepherd, Jesus protects us from the devil. (*Smile.*) When (*Look around at children. You are about to make a point a child has great interest in!*) we are scared, we can take our fears to Jesus. He will make us feel better!

"So, the next time (*Hold up picture again for all the children to see.*) you see a picture of a shepherd, remember that Jesus is our Shepherd. He takes care of us!" *Lay picture or closed book down in your lap.*)

Prayer

"Dear Jesus, thank You for being our Shepherd. Please help us to let You take care of us. In Jesus' name we pray. Amen."

25

Follow the Leader

Remember the Lord in everything you do. And he will give you success.—**Proverbs 3:6**

Object Needed: None. It is good, occasionally, to have nothing in your hands, for the unusual is always an attention getter! This ploy should be used, however, only occasionally.

"Good morning!" (*You.*)
"Good morning!" (*Their response.*)
"This morning we are (*Look around at the children.*) going to talk about (*Smile.*) a children's game! This game is called 'Follow the Leader.' I want you to raise you hand if you've ever played 'Follow the Leader.' (*Repeat. Then look around briefly and see how many hands are raised. Ignore all verbal responses.*) That's nice!" (*This comment pats them on the head emotionally and makes them feel like you really understand them.*)
"We know that when we play 'Follow the Leader,' we are supposed to do only what the leader wants us to do—or we lose the game. (*Repeat from "we are supposed" on.*) Well, the same thing is true of life. If we want to win at life, we have to do only what God wants us to do." (*Repeat.*)
(*Wrinkle your brow and frown.*) "Why is God our Leader? (*You don't want a verbal response, so keep talking.*) Because God is God. God never lets anything happen without a reason. God always wants what's best for us, and God never makes mistakes. If we follow God as our Leader, we will win at life! The Bible tells us, in Proverbs 3:6, 'Remember the Lord in everything you do. And he will give you success.' (*Repeat.*) So, the next time you play 'Follow the Leader,' remember that God is our Leader!"

Prayer
"Dear God, thank You for being God. Please help us remember to do only what You would have us do. In Jesus' name we pray. Amen."

26

The Most Important Verse in the Bible

For God loved the world so much that he gave his only Son. God gave his Son so that whoever believes in him may not be lost, but have eternal life.—**John 3:16**

Object Needed: A picture of Jesus wrapped up in a gift box that can be easily unwrapped. Have a tag on the outside that says, "To You."

(*Walk in carrying gift box. Sit down and put box in your lap.*)
"Good morning!" (*You.*)
"Good morning!" (*Their response.*)
"This morning (*Smile.*) we are going to talk about the most important verse (*Make your eyes big.*) in the whole Bible! (*Repeat, looking around at the children.*) This verse is John 3:16. The verse says, 'For God loved the world so much that he gave his only Son. God gave his Son so that whoever believes in him may not be lost, but have eternal life.'

"God gave to us because He loves us so much! He loves us so much He doesn't want us to have to hurt. 'Whoever believes in' God's Son Jesus will be able to live in Heaven forever! (*Repeat. Then point with index finger for emphasis as you say the next sentence.*) Now, suppose (*Call by name and point to a child most of*

47

the other children will recognize.) Jim and I are friends, and we like to play games together. But suppose one day Jim does something bad, (*There will be giggles and snickers here, but don't stop. You want them to get into your point.*) and his father says he'd going to spank him. (*NOTE: If you are a woman, choose a female child and have her mother want to spank her.*) Then suppose I tell Jim's father, 'Yes, (*Nod your head.*) Jim has been bad and he deserves to be spanked. But (*Shake your head.*) I love him, and I don't want to see him hurt. I want you to spank me instead.'"

(*At this point, you'll have their riveted attention, because the idea you've just proposed is, in their minds, incredible. Pause briefly to let it really sink in. Then proceed.*) "Well, that's exactly what God did. He loves us so much He sent Jesus to hurt in our place. Because Jesus died on a cross, and then (*Turn your hand palm up and raise it.*) rose from the dead, (*Smile.*) we can live forever in Heaven!

"So, the next time you think about God, remember that He loves us so much, He gave (*Put both hands on gift box.*) us (*Hold up tag for all to see. Then open gift box and take out picture of Jesus and hold it up for all the children to see.*) Jesus." (*Pause briefly as children look at picture and really take in the most important thing you'll ever tell them. Then lower picture gently onto your lap as you finish talking.*)

Prayer
"Dear God, thank You for loving us so much. Please help us as we believe in Jesus. In Jesus' name we pray. Amen."